A Special Place
for Charlee

A Child's Companion Through Pet Loss

By
Debby Morehead

Illustrated by Karen Cannon

©1996 PARTNERS IN PUBLISHING, LLC.

A portion of the proceeds from the sale of this book will be donated to Morris Animal Foundation.

Morris Animal Foundation is a nonprofit organization that improves the health and well-being of companion animals and wildlife by funding humane animal health studies and disseminating information about these studies. Founded in 1948 by Mark L. Morris, DVM, the Foundation has sponsored more than 680 animal health studies with funds exceeding $14.4 million. These studies advance the diagnosis, treatment and prevention of diseases and illnesses of dogs, cats, horses, llamas, mountain gorillas as well as other wildlife.

Many animal enthusiasts support the Foundation. One hundred percent of unrestricted, annual donations support programs, not administration. To find out how you can support Morris Animal Foundation call toll-free (800) 243-2345, or write: 45 Inverness Drive East, Englewood, CO 80112.

Frisbee® is a brand name and registered trademark of Mattel, Inc., used by permission.

Text and illustrations copyright © 1996 by Partners in Publishing, LLC

Partners in Publishing, LLC
1074 East 17th Avenue, Broomfield, CO 80020
(303) 466-7724

Printed in USA.
Book design and illustrations by Karen Cannon
Library of Congress Catalog Number 96-92552
Morehead, Debby. A Special Place for Charlee—A Child's Companion Through Pet Loss

1. Children and death—Juvenile literature   2. Bereavement—Juvenile literature
3. Pets—Death—Psychological aspects—Juvenile literature. {1. Pets—Death   2. Death}
4. Veterinary—Pet loss—Psychological aspects   5. Human-Animal Bonding

ISBN 0-9654049-0-0

I wish to express my love and appreciation to my husband, **David Morehead, DVM**, for your love, encouragement, and support; to my children, **Lora** and **Mark** for your inspiration; my family and friends, **Mary Allen-Owings**, **Donna Williams**, **Sandy** and **Bruce Vincent**, and **Shirley Dowling** for your help and belief in me; and business partner, **Mark Abusamra** for helping make my idea become a reality.

Special thanks to: **Dr. Rob Hilsenroth**, **Dr. James F. Wilson**, and **Elise Wilson**, and **Dr. Karen Boland**, for their encouragement and praise of the book, and **Laurel Lagoni**, for her enthusiastic help in providing professional insights and guidance on grief counseling. To **Karen Cannon**, I want to express my gratitude for her sensitive, artistic talent that captures the love and emotions of my story through her illustrations.

And finally, I want to thank a special dog named **Charlee** who gave the Morehead family many wonderful years of unconditional love and memories we will always treasure.

Debby Morehead

"Mark, you spelled Charlie's name wrong!" my friends would say every time they looked at my dog's collar. I would laugh and tell them how my Mom and Dad had gone to an animal shelter before I was born and picked out this big, floppy-eared dog. Mom took one look at the dog and name "him" Charlie. When they discovered "he" was a girl, Mom said, "No problem. Her name is still Charlie, we'll just spell it CHARLEE."

By the time I was born, Charlee was an important member of the family. Dad said Charlee helped teach me important things, like how to crawl around on the floor, how to "shake off" when you get wet, and how much fun it is to play with Frisbee discs.

Charlee and I were best friends. She slept on my bed. I knew I could always count on her. When Mom and Dad got mad at me and sent me to my room, Charlee would come with me and lay her head on my lap. She always loved me, no matter what I did.

On our family camping trips, Charlee and I would head straight for the lake. She loved the water. When I would throw sticks in the lake, she would jump in and bring them back to me. Then she would stand right beside me to "shake off" so I would get wet, too! We had a great time together.

When I was seven, Mom and I took Charlee to the veterinarian for her regular check-up and shots. Since we had taken her every year, Dr. Moore could see that Charlee was starting to show her age. She gave us lots of information on how to take care of an older dog and said if we had any problems or questions to call her.

Over the next few years I began to see changes in Charlee. She still loved to go on walks and play catch with her Frisbee, but she would get tired and have to stop and rest. She started having trouble going up and down stairs. Even her bright eyes got sort of cloudy-looking.

We took Charlee in for check-ups more often and Dr. Moore took very good care of her. Dr. Moore did everything she could to keep Charlee healthy and happy. It hurt me to see how much Charlee tried to do everything we had always done together, but just couldn't. Instead, she wanted to sleep most of the time and seemed to be happiest when I would just sit beside her and pet her.

Early one Saturday morning a strange noise woke me up. Charlee was lying on my bed coughing. She seemed to have trouble breathing. I ran to Mom and Dad's room to tell them something was really wrong with Charlee. Mom called Dr. Moore while Dad and I carried Charlee to the car. I held Charlee's head and hugged her all the way to the animal hospital. I felt scared and so sad. All I could do was cry. I kept telling her how much I loved her.

Dr. Moore met us at the animal hospital. She examined Charlee and told us Charlee's heart had failed. Dad, Mom, and I talked about what we could do that would be the best for Charlee. We were all crying when we asked Dr. Moore to euthanize her. It was the hardest decision I had ever been a part of but I just couldn't stand to see her suffer. Dr. Moore put her arm around my shoulder and said, "Mark, I know how hard it is to lose such a special friend. When I was ten, my dog died and I cried and cried."

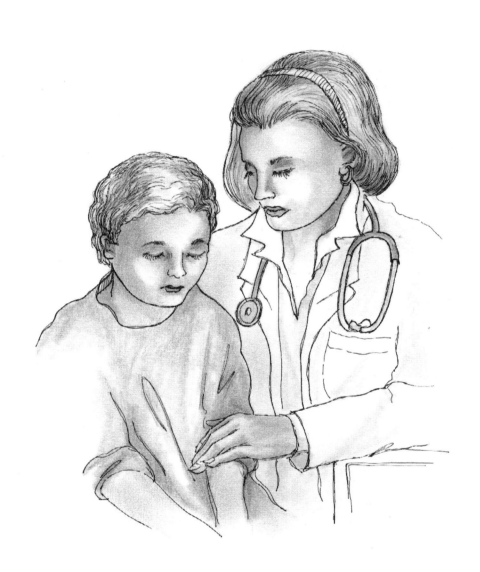

Everyone who worked at the animal hospital was very sad. They told us how much they liked Charlee. Mom, Dad and I hugged each other, cried, and said good-bye to our special friend.

As we were leaving, Dr. Moore told me it was important to share my feelings with my Mom and Dad, because talking to someone you love can help you feel better. She told us to call her if we needed any help. I could tell she was really sad.

That night, Mom sat with me in my room until I went to sleep because she knew I would be lonely without Charlee on my bed.

It took time for the sadness and loneliness to go away. One thing we did to help ourselves feel better was to pick a special time one afternoon to sit in the backyard and remember Charlee. We called it Our Memorial To The Best Dog In the World! The three of us talked about all the funny things she did. We laughed, cried, and hugged each other. Mom suggested we get all of our pictures of Charlee and make a scrapbook about her. She asked me if I wanted to write down some of my special memories of Charlee for the scrapbook. I thought it was a good idea. We also bought a pretty flowering bush and planted it near Charlee's favorite place to lie in the backyard. Dad said the bush would always remind us of her.

For awhile, even after our memorial, I felt like life was going to be sad forever. Sometimes, along with feeling sad, I also felt mad. It wasn't fair that Charlee had to get old and die. Other times I just felt lonely, knowing she wasn't with me anymore.

At first, my friends were sorry when they found out Charlee had died, but before long, they seemed to forget about her. They wondered why I was still so sad. One day when I said I didn't feel like playing, one of the guys even said, "Mark, it was just a dog, get over it!" It made me mad so I told them all to go home. They all left except my next door neighbor, Lora. She was a year older and seemed to understand how I felt.

She sat down beside me and said, "Charlee wasn't just a dog, she was your best friend!" After she said that, I was glad she had stayed. I told her life was just not the same without Charlee. Lora said she knew what I meant. Her cat, Sam, had died the year before. He had been hit by a car. "I was so sad. I did not want to eat much or do anything but sit in my room and think about Sam. I put a special picture of Sam on the table beside my bed. I talked to his picture a lot and said how bad I felt that he wasn't with me anymore. I even kept Sam's old beat-up toy under my pillow at night so I would feel close to him."

I told Lora my Mom and Dad had asked me if we should get another dog. They said they knew we could never replace Charlee, but they would like to have a new pet someday. I understood how my parents felt but I just wasn't ready for a new dog. Lora nodded and said, "It took me a long time to want to have a new cat." Just then her new cat jumped down off the backyard fence. She came over and laid down in Lora's lap to be petted. "I thought no cat in the world could be as good as Sam. I was afraid if I loved a new cat it wouldn't be fair to Sam. But one day I went with my Dad to the Humane Society and started playing with a cute little kitten. I realized that nothing would ever make me forget how much I loved Sam nor all the good memories I had of him. I found a special place to keep my love and memories of Sam. It will take some time, but you will find a special place to keep your love and memories of Charlee."

A few days later, as I walked by the park, I saw a girl throwing a Frisbee to her dog. I thought, "Charlee used to jump up in the air for a Frisbee just like that dog." Then something strange happened. I remembered how much fun Charlee and I used to have playing Frisbee in the park. When I thought about Charlee, instead of feeling sad and lonely I smiled and felt good!

When I got home I found Dad in the kitchen. I told him how I had felt in the park and how good it was to be able to be happy again.

Late that afternoon I saw Lora in her backyard. I waved and she said, "Hi Mark, how are you doing?"

"I'm better," I said. "I still miss Charlee a lot, but I know she will always be with me. I found that special place you told me about where I will keep all my love and memories of Charlee ...

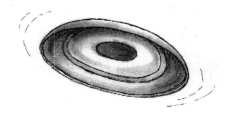

IN MY HEART."